THE VERBS OF DESIRING

THE VERBS OF DESIRING

poems by

Renée Ashley

new american press

Fort Collins, Colo.

new american press

© 2010 by Renée Ashley

Printed in the United States of America

ISBN 978-0-9817802-5-2

For ordering information, please visit
www.NewAmericanPress.com

Some poems in this book first appeared in *Chautauqua Literary Review*, *Colorado Review*, *Columbia*, *Columbia Poetry Review*, *Connecticut Review*, *Field*, *Greensboro Review*, *Iodine*, *Kenyon Review*, *The Literary Review*, *Schuylkill Valley Journal of the Arts*, *Tiferet*, *U.S. 1*, and *versedaily.com*.

"A Wind Is Like So Many Arrows A House Like So Many Some Kind Of Doors" and "Wine Not Water Fish Not Frogs" were first published in *POETRYETC: Poems & Poets*, edited by Andrew Burke and Candice Ward, and "I Have a Theory About Reflection" won the *Greensboro Review* Robert Watson Literary Prize.

CONTENTS

For Arthur Earl Jones

and Barney Schweyer

my love and more words

a desire of a different be

THE VERBS OF DESIRING

THE VERBS OF DESIRING

How tired the self is of self, its earth twirling in the air and
not-air and I know a woman who ate only bread until
                                    she died
of bread. Oh the where-is-she-now. Which is not a question.
Which is a noun of circumstance.
                        And *disquietude*: lovely
word. And *hairsbreadth. Stupor mundi. Kettle-of-fish-that-
turned-your-heart.*
                    You are returning from an alphabet ran-
sacked by thirst, by the gamut of implication neatly sung:
a tongue that speaks
                    body. A punctuated earth. You who are
resolute of hungry brutes and fooled by the beggar's bowl of
moon, tide of scat, of pellet and flop
                            and the body's dead-
end is an assured apostrophe.
                        There are more ways to mean
than you can make note of.
                        Look! Something is pretty in the sky
– it might just be the sky – though installation's been askant.
Or what it sits upon is opposed to the level eye.
                            A panoply of
possibilities –
                all those bears pirouetting in your penthouse!
Oh if it or they were only.
                        Or if you. And, or if I.

AND TAKEN

A backward breath into lung and recall – I know what damage is. I know the gun, trigger of the heart. Respire. Expire. Aback or away. The day has been all eyes and all those open. You are in me like too many mouths.

WHOSE BRIGHT EXAMINING

You go anyway so. What do they call you? chucklehead?
dickbender? bowl of fish? skeet? (At this rate the woman

will never ah! she's forgotten the beginning the end.)
They drew a chalk shadow in the shape of the female

not the dog. Head hanging like a flag. (You have to say
what you think no you don't you never have to say that

out loud.) Not one shifts an impulse onto the bright with
her in mind. (One makes a soft, simple sound in the creak

of the attic roof. In the sink spilling over.) Such mewing
and crying! Love makes you stupid you still don't get it

you are not the world you're barely there. So. The light
on those gravestones still takes the shape of gravestones

and the dog whispers (the dog *never*) bone of the center.
Bone of the grass. God! (How can you not understand?

You carry the living. The heart laboring hard in its cell.
Mother of all things unfruitful. Victim of everything.)

OH YES TOMORROW EXPECT THE ORDINARY

The dogs sing beautifully over everything beautiful
or not – white sleet or white sun -- and you have never
yet begun with nothing. Tell your friends to wait. This
will take some time. Imagine a burned house – steamy
sill, dampened ash. Shingle, lintel, coal. An emptiness

spread like soot. Can you even begin to comprehend
nothing? Posit a negative in a positive mind, the idea
of no idea expanding? The dark smell of *gone*, of *you
can't get this back.*   Consider the stark break between
yes and *so often* – between *no* and *not yet*, *some time.*

Think *hypothetical, absolute.* Oh druggery! Oh *get me
through this.* Every day. Dog song and dander jig your
approach -- such joy! Privilege and you so heart-poor.
A poverty of fire. You yourself consumed. But not so
simple. Never as clear as that. Nothing so sweetly entire.

A GUN IS NOT DISCURSIVE

(This time) it is a woman who lies it is
the woman who last night said *you are*
safe with me I do not lie. In a darkened
room such light can take out your eyes

the heart's box is broken. Fib as big as
an apple down your throat and the spine's
tree heating up, hope's rondo spinning in
your brain. Silly you. No one's endearment

is tidy. The garden? A huge dried-up lot.
And the body grateful for unlikely waters.

NOTHING LESS THAN LESS THAN NOTHING

You have forgotten the words you need
to say that. (You've misplaced articles

: things are dangling, things are running
on, your restrictive clause is on the rails

in a universe parallel & sadly contracted.)
Your madmen are useless. (You liked me

best when I could not speak.) Your friends
say they're deaf -- and the ringing in your

ears is real. You've bum-rushed every one
who's tried to love you (they tend to leave

in the most abrupt ways). You're alone be-
cause you scoured your house with sorrow.

Your daily word is *cry* (words have never
had meaning until now). Write your rebuke

in the white space around you, in what
could be called *sleep* or *that-which-is-like*,

the saying of what might really matter, of
what, so surely, you never will utter at all.

ALLEGORY OF THE MYTH
OF THE SEEMINGLY COMPLEX ONLY

because it's on your mind: cowlick of moon
bright spittle that swings at the lip of an easy

and night the dark thing that stares past you
elegant equipoise and the unwagered self – oh

what would the truth have been? (She carries
the Drowned Man in a paper sack the Hanged

Man in a cardboard cup there's a lantern in her
throat a length of twine a bolt) Oh there must be

order so blessèd be each Puzzle-breaker Doll-
shaker Trouble-taker Cake-baker Thing-Be-

yond-Sorrow that falls like dust from the beams
(She dressed him in a little tuxedo – no sleeves –

on his dick like dressing a thumb for the ball) Or
the story of might-have-happened sordid history

of the pelvic boat the furnace great well of every-
thing (She forgets her life half-lived down a crap-

strewn road one mile or two away lit by a spit of
stars) of tell me how to read this poem Absolutely

has (Her hand the troubled weathers) Ah Must be
A principle of progression A rubric of simplicity

I RUN TO THE SAD MAN IN THE WHITE CAR AND

This is a different gun, reader, than you have heard about
before. From me. This is a different tragedy. The man in
the white car is weary of sorrow weary the way a woman
becomes weary of a man. Or of her life. (Or of a satchel
which might contain the whole history a whole of sorrow's
vestige.) This man is learning the gun: singed wing, orphan,
rare bird. Sorrow can fly and a gun can fly and a shot. And
time. But time is simply metaphor here & hardly a metaphor
at all. Not flying. Dragging a busted wing, dragging its bitter.
(Like a satchel.) Dragging its stark and dragging its bleak,
dragging its heavy its carcass its blasted-out carrion heart.

THERE IS A WOMAN WAITING FOR SOMEONE TO TELL HER THE TRUTH

There is a woman built of questions and she is broken
and there is a hole in her head the size of her mother's
head there is a hole in her head the size of her father's
wound and the dogs sniffle and fart their warm wishes
they bite they bark their huzzahs they sing there's a man
out there too and a house with dirty windows that she
loves. She's not ready to swap (she's lying) the slender
skill of being alive. The finite barter of staying that way.

WHAT IS VISIBLE IS WHAT MOSTLY IS

So this too is no longer a poem about the bat
in the opera house and not that other one either.
Nothing *Fleder--*. Nothing *–maus*. Not the brown
one in the roof beams spreading its fingery wings;
not the long-handled net we catch it in. What is
visible is what mostly is. A relic, one small figment
of fractured bone. No thing is holy or ever will be.
Look: some of all the ways you could get caught:
water under water or the earth beneath all that.

HOW TO PUT IT

The fragment as spoken by the one lost. His heart singing in
its dish.

The dish breaking beneath his heart's singing. Down by the
reservoir

cars slide into the darkening water. The moon's pull does not
save them.

In daylight in the parking lot of the market three miles away
the gray birds

will not move for the car; the one-legged birds stand on their
one leg.

The world is not broken. The world is local. Singing in its
spinning dish.

Its song, wordless, is rondo. Oh, just listen: it comes comes
comes again.

A WIND IS LIKE SO MANY ARROWS A HOUSE LIKE SO MANY SOME KIND OF DOORS

It's more complicated than that. Metaphor
or not it's this one body breaking up sends
the mind's bear scrambling in the pit. Self
is a rugged low-down thing, time's loaded.
Poor mind. Poor bear. Poorest hour of end:
the winds are up, foreclosures. Every place
you look eyesore and bellyflop, the single
imperfect discourse of an unfinished world.

NEITHER THE COCK ON FIRE
NOR THE TIN ROOF BANGING

And that is not the barking of pigs you hear.
The spleen-angels are wrangling in the garden again.
Listen, there's no need for upset. It's what
they do. What they are best at. The angels
are experts. Are doing their job. Trust them—
I know it's hard to see. And the brouhaha stops you.
Not even drunks caterwaul like that. Feral critters
have better manners. So, walk past first, then turn,
look over your shoulder. The light is better that way.

You'll have to listen past the growling.
The angels are calling your name. They
know what you're thinking. They're sitting
at your table. They're wearing your cast-off clothes.

STARS WHEN I FIRST SAW IT

Scrap of glimmer, dab of soot – puff of never was. Nothing
left behind overhead below. Here is what can be made, what

can be unmade. (A father is an ice man luggage hauler ball
bearing maker. Mother a hinge a hammer a hasp.) No thing

can be saved from nothing (not a thing said to be lost). Here
is the hand that knows subtraction. (Cut it off.) The blue eye

that speaks one blue from blue (not permitted put it out) – and
night's the edge and day a trail of lighter blue at the edge's

edge. The mouth that tells this has a tongue twice split – traitor
liar not-be-there not-see. (Oh.) I was stars when I first saw it.

THROWN TO THE AWAY

I seem to know this: at once you
fell towards the river towards

the startled space between us, body
at its very rest, its irresolute edge listing

and thrown to the away. Undertow is
the current in between. It pulls at

what is left behind. The other. The
dust. All the evidence you ever were.

SIMPLE

and the whole white sky descends a grain
at a time – I with it and the threshold dis-

appearing. That we can find ourselves
in this. That some thing might sigh so

artless an exhalation (*storm* the oddest word
for early, unearned sweetness, for blinded

panes -- brown dogs over their heads in blue
snow, their red hearts clanging, their eyes

as good as sightless except for the joy. For
the loss of that other, a better known world).

SPINDLE, LATHE

Thirst rose in her from a sitting position.
There was *would this* and *would that.*

There was the man. Not as she thought.
Was the lick. Was the try. When she saw

the sky was broken. When locked her
simple door. Her tongue put out like

so little fire. The what was left. Spindle,
lathe. Latch. The heart like two barn doors.

I HAVE A THEORY ABOUT REFLECTION

I cannot put my mother in the freezer and neither can I store
her in the attic nor in the bank box nor in the canister of sugar
In fact she is calling me now she is ringing in my kitchen in
both bedrooms in the upstairs office I am wearing her like a
too-big coat The coat is made of wire I shoo her away I flap
my hands: *go away go away* I am a match and every time we
speak – and sometimes when we do not – she strikes me Even
in the bend of a spoon I can see her reaching

MY FATHER IS ASHES

We are electric I know our conductor He is a very sad man
We are not in a field of cosmos We are not in a field I'm only
telling you that when the message leaves the body I do not
know what to make of the world I make you up from the little
I know with almost with soon Is it possible the thing I love
most is guilt or that you are gone We are such pain and we
are utterance We are a strange thing in the air You are so
imperfectly dead

BODIES IN INCREMENTS BODIES IN WHOLES

We are close to listening and these are stories out of what is
At the entry to day and night my darling says *the dead are
always bringing up the past* and *every view is just one view* Before
me the twins were aborted For me the dog was put down The
rabbit was stew Hard not to wager abstraction after that Not
blame but a six-pack of consequence of recognition I say
observation dilutes image It must I can do no more than this
We are the indefinite article

MOSTLY THERE IS, MOSTLY I DO

i

To live, you must row across the mother. How
good it is to go away; how good not to go back
again. Imagine the air around a bell, how it is
displaced the way the city sets a fire in the sky
and burns. Imagine the heart folded like a bedsheet.
Her glass letters. Everything grounded in the pelvic
boat: our lady of the pipe dream, lady of perpetual
disappointment. The landscape of ropes in the blue
story twinning and taking her the dark way home –
a life stacked like wood, the uninfinite self still
by itself with the unfounded rumors of simplicity.

ii

You can't even count the times you've told the story:
the father, the sound of no response at all, the white car,
and then racing the ambulance home. No sea to cross
for the father, no trope to carry his body back to the husk
of a house in the mountains. Just the gun, the blossom
of red above his ear. Undertakers who do a piss-poor job,
the bared head seeping on the satin. A sea of nothing but
minus while the skull hollows itself. And regret having
petals. Or, as well, an ocean's worth of recognition: lights
out, water running, a not-quite-on-the-mark precipitous blast.
Your grandmother's name was Crick. No relation. And what

is relation anyway? Blood running through a corridor.
A swinging gate. You will die but you hope not drown
or burn. You hope sleep takes you with your laundry done.
You hope your shame – big as a mountain top – dies with
you, that it doesn't rest visible and polished on the mantel
like a loving cup or small casket of ash with a plaque
of attribution. You don't know who you are but for that
small thing only you will name – and you would not pass
that on. You have been careful not to pass that on. You
throw the windows open, the doors, toss the drapes out,
batter the rugs; you hope the wind will clean your house.

PAIN

Would like to place it in a town Or a state
of this unknown union But no A state yes and
of too much being And weather a slide rule of
weather The body a forecast of pain so much
like love the contract of sorrow if you will Even
if you won't Even if you want out And always
never say always someone worse so complaint
which of course this is becomes unbecoming But
unbecoming is what all this is about   Sleep if
you're lucky if you've got the small round goods
Some other state with the sun's eyes closed yours
too (can't live on metaphor) Are all but persuaded
to say the word *die* you are so willing to die

HAMMER AND NAIL

Head of both hammer and nail,
  the blunt, blunt, blunt un-

attributable strike, an altered
  line in the midst of the banging.

It's beginning to show. The crack
  quickened by contact, by fleet

and nasty (oh need), by burn.
  By stifle. The jangling taste

of metal in the mouth. The teeth
  too heavy to raise – so the break

in the breath in the bowels in the
  center that sorts your moments.

I consider the devils I own:
  they wear women's clothes.

IF THE BODY

If the body is an object? cracked
   like a pot that cannot hold

its swill? Consider the ties to
   matter. (*Begin the poem with a*

predicament. Write what you
   know.) Have a little fall-down

-- plenty of space and no one to tell
   the neighbors. A nifty room and

a view of the dead who have a view
   of you. We are riding an island.

East wind is a cleaner of houses;
   old ships bring back bad news.

ESSAY ON OBSERVATION

The crows gather low in the trees at the woodland's
edge, barking their throaty wisdoms, unsettling their
flared, black wings. Squirrels hurry to gather beneath

their shade just before -- against gravity -- they stream
back upward nearer the pending havoc. The deer and

the bear have gone. The woodchuck. The poor creeping
vole. The crippled chipmunk gone back to his rock wall
for his short life. The toads are hiding beneath their stones;

the air is violet with what hasn't yet arrived. Brown
dog and black dog are crazy-eyed and lather-tongued,

thunder barreling from the west, and flat against
the neighbor's bouldered rampart, is someone's yellow
cat, nearly dwarfed by the cowbird rigid in its mouth --

not struck, but stunned, by that first galvanic flash, so
near it appears to have cut her joy in two. The air swells,

is nickel, then silver with rain -- soon white with a down-
pour that beats the caladiums into the earth, Rose of Sharon
onto its knees, a whole world coming down onto the world.

AN ART LIKE ANY OTHER

Take a woman who has no child and give her a child—like
that!—and she thinks: *more than me more than all of you.* It's
beautiful. But of course it doesn't happen that way. You never
wanted it to happen that way. You know your heart is a mis-
take. You are the woman bringing nothing driving in the se-
miotic fog. The city is wearing its shroud: you are an elephant,
a pearl. You are as right as a gate. You are hidden in your
bone nest when you hear it: a young man restless at an inter-
section speaking to a silver phone: *No, no. Not embarrassed,* he
says. *I just didn't want to wake up next to you.* He's not speaking
to you; you're thankful for that. Because you know when he
says *I love you* her heart closes—bam!—like a window falling
shut. She says her heart is not a window, it is a store and the
store is closed. And nobody knows how the heart stores what
it knows. We know the other truth. We know the sky is frayed
and that the beginning begins here. Every time. The body has
its say: *I can do that for you.* It says: *You are building the moun-
tain you fall from.* And you are undone in the air. It says *An art
like any other.* There must be a word for this but you do not
have a speaking part. Because you are not the same. As before.
Because no one was at hand to say *Please don't go.*

WINE NOT WATER FISH NOT FROGS

Everything in the garden of the world. The small
cup of her. Gratitude and those birds pulling down

the sky. What weighs most on a god's scale -- other
than a god? My mother told me her first father killed

her other father. I found this in a note, it's my writing
– she did not tell me how. Or I've forgotten again.

From here all I can see is roofs but I can hear the sea.
Hear birds in the inlet three doors down but the sky

seems stable. They appear to do no harm. The question
can't be: Who will know when she's gone? It's frogs

and fishes. It's atumble, askew, atip in the midden. I've
learned not to find truth in a world. I'm trying to go on.

Renée Ashley has received several awards for her work, including the Ruth Lake Memorial and Robert H. Winner Awards from the Poetry Society of America; the Award for Emerging Writers and the Award for Literary Excellence, both from the *Kenyon Review*; the 1996 *Chelsea* Award in Poetry; the 1997 *American Literary Review* Award in Poetry; and Fellowships from the New Jersey State Council on the Arts and the National Endowment for the Arts. Her collection *Salt* won the Brittingham Prize in Poetry (Univ. of Wisconsin Press, 1991) and her collection *Basic Heart* won the X. J. Kennedy Prize in Poetry (Texas Review Press, 2009). Her other books include *The Various Reasons of Light* (Avocet Press, 1998), *The Revisionist's Dream* (Avocet Press, 2001), and *Someplace Like This*, a novel (Permanent Press, 2003).